RAND

Attracting "Cutting-Edge" Skills Through Reserve Component Participation

Gregory F. Treverton, David Oaks, Lynn Scott, Justin L. Adams

Prepared for the
Office of the Secretary of Defense

National Defense Research Institute

The research described in this report was sponsored by the Office of the Secretary of Defense (OSD). The research was conducted in RAND's National Defense Research Institute, a federally funded research and development center supported by the OSD, the Joint Staff, the unified commands, and the defense agencies under Contract DASW01-01-C-0004.

Library of Congress Cataloging-in-Publication Data

Attracting "cutting-edge" skills through reserve component participation / Gregory F. Treverton ... [et at.].
      p. cm.
   "MR-1729."
   ISBN 0-8330-3445-6 (pbk.)
      1. United States—Armed Forces—Reserves. 2. United States—Armed Forces—Recruiting, enlistment, etc. 3. Manpower—United States. 4. Military readiness—United States. I. Treverton, Gregory F.

UA42.A88 2003
355.2'23'0973—dc21

                                                                                   2003014361

RAND is a nonprofit institution that helps improve policy and decisionmaking through research and analysis. RAND® is a registered trademark. RAND's publications do not necessarily reflect the opinions or policies of its research sponsors.

Published 2003 by RAND
1700 Main Street, P.O. Box 2138, Santa Monica, CA 90407-2138
1200 South Hayes Street, Arlington, VA 22202-5050
201 North Craig Street, Suite 202, Pittsburgh, PA 15213-1516
RAND URL: http://www.rand.org/
To order RAND documents or to obtain additional information, contact Distribution Services: Telephone: (310) 451-7002; Fax: (310) 451-6915; Email: order@rand.org

Preface

This report describes the results of a project done for the Office of the Secretary of Defense, Reserve Affairs (RA) entitled "Developing Hard to Grow Skills Through Reserve Component Participation." The purpose of the project was to develop ideas for innovatively using the Reserve Component (RC) to provide the military access to skill sets that it would have difficulty recruiting and retaining in the usual ways. The project team scanned a wide variety of ideas and, in consultation with the sponsor, developed five ideas in some detail.

The report is intended to make the results of that exploration available not just to RA and to other Department of Defense officials who manage the Reserve Component but also to others, inside and outside government, who are concerned about the difficulty the military and the government as a whole will have recruiting and retaining many of the skills they will need in an increasingly specialized world. It is the latest of a long series of RAND analyses of manpower and personnel issues, for both the Reserve and Active Components.

This research was conducted within the Forces and Resources Policy Center of RAND's National Defense Research Institute, a federally funded research and development center sponsored by the Office of the Secretary of Defense, the Joint Staff, the unified commands, and the defense agencies. Comments are welcome and may be addressed to the project leader, Gregory Treverton, at gregt@rand.org. For more information on RAND's Forces and Resources Policy Center, contact the director, Susan Everingham, susan_everingham@rand.org, 310-393-0411, extension 7654.

Contents

Figure

Tables

Summary

This report focuses on one critical slice of the ways the Reserve Component (RC) makes needed skills available to the Active Component (AC): attracting "cutting-edge" skills. We define *cutting-edge skills* as those that are

- complex, therefore time-consuming and expensive to train

- generally either not produced in large numbers or, as in information technology (IT) and other engineering fields, subject to "boom and bust" cycles, periodically making them in scarce supply for the military

- primarily developed and used in the civilian world, but less frequently or intermittently used in the military world (for instance, linguists, area specialists, information system designers)

- generally without a long-term career development path or even requirement within the military

- difficult to keep current. For instance, the military is normally a consumer of rapid technological advances but only infrequently a producer; specific language skills are infrequently used in the military and are hence hard to maintain

- often not tightly connected to the combat components of the military

- needed quickly in a crisis. The military cannot wait for months or years to obtain such skills when war or international crisis is imminent.

IT specialists are the most often cited example of cutting-edge skills. Specialists in unusual languages are another: Their skills may be obsolete if not used and may be quickly needed, but they will not be developed or sought by the private sector in large numbers.

In thinking about how to attract such skills into the RC, we examined a wide range of policy ideas. In the end, we focused on five policy ideas that seem both worthwhile and feasible:

1. Civilian Skills Database

2. Expanded "Participating IRR" (Individual Ready Reserve)

3. "Tailored" ESGR (Employer Support to Guard and Reserve)

4. RC-Focused PaYS (Partnership for Youth Success)

5. Critical University Talent Program.

This report analyzes each in terms of difficulty, cost, and attractiveness to those with cutting-edge skills. We describe the ideas briefly here. (The analysis is summarized in Table S.1 on page xiv.)

1. **Database of Skills Possessed by Existing RC Members, Especially Those in the IRR.** The best place to start in harnessing skills in the RC is with the skills that are already present. But databases used by RC managers generally contain, at most, the current civilian occupation of service members. They are neither timely (occupation information is rarely updated), broad (only one occupation can be maintained in most databases), nor deep (what kind of programs can this software engineer write?).

   Better databases could produce a relatively short-term "win-win" situation. This initiative would draw on databases already being developed by the RC—Joint Reserve Intelligence Planning Support System (JRIPSS), Army Reserve Civilian Acquired Skills Database (CASDB), Naval Reserve Skills Online, and related systems—to provide a basis for eventual transfer to the Defense Integrated Military Human Resources System (DIMHRS). The most difficult part of the task is getting service members to enter and update data. A variety of incentives could be offered, from exhortation to pay for one training period.

2. **Expanded "Participating IRR."** This program, based on an existing Air Force program, would aim to identify, track, and reward a subset of IRR members who want to serve. They could be given particular incentives—perhaps pay, but also training opportunities or health, retirement, or other non-salary benefits, although some of these non-salary benefits, health care in particular, can be expensive. Particular cutting-edge skills, such as foreign language or technology skills, might be special targets. Participating IRR members would not be counted against unit strengths or ceilings.

3. **"Tailored" ESGR.** This program would build on the basic structure of the existing ESGR but would seek to foster more and better connections to employers. The ESGR organization may provide the fastest and most effective means to access these critical, cutting-edge resources. It understands the constraints of both the employer's willingness and ability to contribute employees and an employee's willingness to participate. In particular, ESGR could enhance the targeting of its message to specific geographical regions, industry sectors, and firms where critical skills reside. Its role would be to

identify the location of specific critical skill talent pools that exist in industry sectors and specific firms within those sectors, and develop comprehensive, targeted marketing strategies to industry leaders, business executives, and people possessing critical skills. ESGR volunteers would then help guide recruiters to talent pools of special interest.

4. **RC-Focused Program Modeled on PaYS.** The Army PaYS program is a partnership between the Army and participating private-sector firms. It is designed to attract young people into the Army who are interested in obtaining high-quality civilian employment after serving their terms of enlistment. During their enlistment in the Army, soldiers learn technical skills required by industry along with work ethic, teamwork, communication, and leadership. After completing their active-duty tour, the soldiers transition to the company selected during the recruiting process. By analogy, a PaYS-like program would be created for the RC in which industry participants agree to hire or give preference to members of the RC. In the program, the RC would maintain basic technical skills, discipline, and training. The RC version of PaYS might be even more attractive to companies because they would not have to wait for participants to serve their active-duty tours.

5. **Critical University Talent Program.** This new initiative would identify colleges and universities that employ faculty and produce graduates at the undergraduate and graduate levels who possess the hard-to-fill, hard-to-train, and hard-to-retain skills that the military needs. It would then identify a specific recruitment pool of faculty and students within these institutions who possess the state-of-the-art science and technical skills or the most current academic knowledge that is sought. It would then develop a retainer-based recruiting and retention program for this talent pool to work within the IRR to fulfill national security needs.

Table S.1 displays the differences among the ideas and the uncertainties about their effects.

The Critical University Talent Program, for instance, seems expensive for the talent it nets. But is it? The only way to answer such a question is to take the logical next step: pilot test the policy ideas to gain a clearer sense of their costs and benefits in terms of attracting desired skill sets. Ideally, those tests would be rigorous, with a control set of cells to assess yield and cost without the new initiative and several other sets implementing the idea in variants along critical dimensions, such as the form or size of the incentive to participate or join the RC.

Table S.1

Cutting-Edge Policy Ideas

	Program				
	Civilian Skills Database	Expanded Partici-pating IRR	"Tailored" ESGR	RC-Focused PaYS	Critical University Talent
Purpose	Identify existing RC members with cutting-edge skills	Encourage more IRR members to participate	Recruit critical skills through companies	Increase number of RC recruits by broker-ing connection to employers	Get critical university-based talent on retainer
Targets	All current RC members	IRR members, especially those with cutting-edge skills	Companies identified as cutting-edge	Non–prior service possible recruits	Federal-grantee university departments
Incentives	Pay for training period Retirement points "Yellow pages"	Pay Retirement points Other non-salary	? More-aggres-sive RC outreach to private sector	Only the chance to interview with companies	Stipends to graduate students and faculty
Yearly program costs	$20–30 million if training pay included	Very dependent on mix of incentives	$5–10 million	$2 million	$20 million for 100 retainers
Number of skill sets produced	4,000?	10,000?	?	? (15,000 might participate)	100?

NOTE: A question mark refers to uncertainties in this area.

[a]See page 10 for an explanation of this concept.

Acknowledgments

We appreciate the very close and helpful cooperation with the project's sponsors, especially Colonel Gary Crone of RA. We also appreciate the time and counsel of a number of people in the various reserve personnel commands and in other reserve activities who helped us develop the idea. They are mentioned in footnotes throughout the report. We had a chance to present our developing ideas to the 2002 Individual Ready Reserve (IRR) Conference, hosted by Army Reserve Personnel Command in St. Louis, and we thank participants for their comments and the Command for its hospitality to interested interlopers. Finally, we have benefited from thoughtful comments by our RAND colleagues, Michael Polich and James Quinlivan, in Polich's case more than once. As usual, though, we thank all these good people but absolve them all from any gremlins that might remain in this report.

Attracting "Cutting-Edge" Skills Through Reserve Component Participation

Framing the Challenge

This report focuses on one critical slice of the ways the Reserve Component (RC) makes needed skills available to the Active Component (AC): attracting "cutting-edge" skills. We define *cutting-edge skills* as those that are

- complex; therefore time-consuming and expensive to train

- generally either not produced in large numbers or, as in information technology (IT) and other engineering fields, subject to "boom and bust" cycles, periodically making them in scarce supply for the military

- primarily developed and used in the civilian world, but less frequently or intermittently used in the military world (for instance, linguists, area specialists, information system designers)

- generally without a long-term career development path or even requirement within the military

- difficult to keep current. For instance, the military is normally a consumer of rapid technological advances but only infrequently a producer; specific language skills are infrequently used in the military and are hence hard to maintain

- often not tightly connected to the combat components of the military

- needed quickly in a crisis. The military cannot wait for months or years to obtain such skills when war or international crisis is imminent.

These skills are "cutting-edge" in the civilian sense of the term, but because they are often removed from the military's "shooters," they might not be thought of as cutting-edge in a military sense. IT specialists are the most often cited example of these skills. Specialists in unusual languages are another. They are not produced in large numbers by the private sector. The military's needs for languages arise quickly: Yesterday, the need was for Russian, Farsi, Spanish, or Somali; today or tomorrow, it may be Chinese, Pashtu, Korean, or Arabic.

As shown in Figure 1, the skills needed by the armed forces might be displayed along two dimensions—the complexity of the skill and the degree to which it

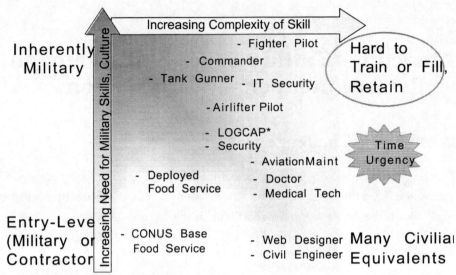

*LOGCAP = Logistics Civil Augmentation Program.

Figure 1—Civilian and Military Skills

requires distinctively military training, experience, and culture. The job titles in the figure are meant only to be suggestive. Both the opportunity to draw on the private sector for cutting-edge skills and the competition with it will be most intense along the right side of the diagram. Many IT skills would be, for instance, in the lower right corner. They are richly present (and, intermittently at least, richly rewarded) in the private sector. However, they may also be easily transferred to the military to the extent that many "military" IT applications are very much like civilian ones, without much need for military understanding, culture, or discipline.

Occupations higher on the right side of the diagram, though, might require both highly developed skills *and* military acculturation and unit cohesion. Special forces units, for instance, have highly skilled communications personnel. They might also need language specialists as translators. To that extent, the technical skills would be cutting-edge, but they would not meet the definition of "cutting-edge" applied here because they could not be moved easily and quickly from civilian jobs to their military counterparts.

The third dimension of the diagram is time. The RC's ability to move people from civilian life to military service in a hurry could be both drawn upon and enhanced. That would provide an argument for using the RC to provide some skills even if the need to wear a uniform were less pressing.

The cutting-edge skills defined here might be better derived from the civilian world—"borrowed" by the military when exigencies demand them. The RC is a much cheaper place to keep those skills than the AC. To be sure, sometimes the skills might simply be contracted for, and that is a complementary option. But using the RC might provide more assurance of getting the needed skills during a crisis than would contracting. And bringing those skills into the RC would afford skill-holders the protections of the uniformed military.

This report is a broad inquiry into how the RC might be used in this manner. At its core are five ideas, meant to be especially relevant to the problem of cutting-edge skills: a Civilian Skills Database; an expanded "Participating IRR" (Individual Ready Reserve) program; a "tailored" Employer Support to Guard and Reserve (ESGR) program; an RC-focused PaYS (Partnership for Youth Success) program; and a Critical University Talent Program.

The report describes what each idea is, why it seems worth pursuing, what the closest existing parallels are, and what key issues remain to be examined in a pilot project or experiment. It also makes preliminary assessments of how hard each idea would be to implement, how much it would cost, and how attractive it might be to its intended targets. In some cases, existing programs provide some analogies for estimating costs (and yields). In others, conversations with existing program managers or potential targets suggest how attractive the idea might be. These judgments are estimates, however, not detailed costing or implementation analyses.

The logical next step is to conduct pilot projects or experiments to test the ideas and refine their features. The final section of the report suggests how that might be done, based on the Army's experiment with the so-called 2+2+4 recruiting program carried out 15 years ago.[1]

Innovations for Meeting Current and Future Skill Needs

Most indicators of personnel shortfalls are, at best, indirect with respect to the challenge of cutting-edge skills. That is because only two of the reasons that shortfalls arise are relevant to the cutting-edge problem: The AC and RC do not attract enough personnel and/or they assign personnel to positions for which they are not trained.[2] (The other reasons for shortfalls are that more personnel

---

[1]See Richard Buddin and Carole E. Roan, *Assessment of Combined Active/Reserve Recruiting Programs* (Santa Monica, CA: RAND, MR-504-A, 1994).

[2]This framework is taken from Michael G. Shanley, Henry A. Leonard, and John D. Winkler, *Army Distance Learning: Potential for Reducing Shortages in Enlisted Occupations* (Santa Monica, CA: RAND, MR-1318-A, 2001).

than authorized are assigned to some occupations, leaving shortages in others, and that assigned personnel may not be available for deployment.)

Examples of accounts of shortfalls are the Army's "Critical MOS List," which documents the Military Occupational Specialties (MOS) with shortages, and the Army Reserve Personnel Command (AR-PERSCOM) Personnel Inventory Management (PIM) Stratification model. This model estimates the shortfall by MOS in the Individual Ready Reserve by estimating the unmet requirements for the Army after accounting for a Presidential Reserve Call-up (PRC) and a Partial Mobilization (PM) of the National Guard to meet a two-major-theater-war scenario.[3]

Viewed from the supply side, shortages in cutting-edge skills may arise in different ways. Some skills are highly specialized and may exist in small quantities in the population because there is a limited industry demand. For example, the skills critical to analyzing the ethnic and cultural complexities surrounding peacekeeping, humanitarian assistance, and counterterrorism missions are possessed by anthropologists, sociologists, historians, foreign language specialists, political scientists, and, in some cases, urban planners. These skills are hard to train because of the depth of knowledge needed for proficiency. In addition, the positions are hard to fill because of the relatively small numbers of people who might posses the specific skill sets that the Department of Defense (DoD) seeks.[4] For instance, of 430,000 master's degrees conferred in the United States in 1998, fewer than 1,700 were in area, ethnic, and cultural studies. Moreover, because the Pentagon has not actively recruited people with these skills, they do not naturally think of the military as a source of employment. And while the military needs to attract them, often on very short notice, it may not need to retain them for their entire career—or even for very long.

Other critical skill sets that are hard to train and hard to recruit are in the physical sciences, science technologies, and communications technologies.[5] Skill sets from these academic areas are more widely sought by the private sector than those from the social sciences. Indeed, the competition is often intense, and the

---

[3]The PRC phase of mobilization is based on the requirements needed in the first 10 to 30 days of mobilization. The PM phase of mobilization is based on the requirements from 40 to 240 days of mobilization. The PRC portion of the model is run first, and then the PM (using the highest requirement among the periods and carrying the shortfall from PRC into PM).

[4]For numbers, see U.S. Department of Education, National Center for Education Statistics, Higher Education General Information Survey (HEGIS), "Degrees and Other Formal Awards Conferred" surveys, and Integrated Postsecondary Education Data System (IPEDS), "Completions" surveys. (This table was prepared in June 2000.)

[5]Skill set titles are taken from the National Center for Education Statistics tables reporting academic degree production at the bachelor's, master's, and doctoral levels.

pool is not large—as measured, for instance, by comparing master's-level graduates in these fields with total master's degrees granted. This is the situation the military faces as it strives for rapid innovations in the creation or employment of command, control, and communication to address new threats or support novel military missions. These innovations may need to come from the leading universities in these discipline areas.

A third group of cutting-edge skills includes computer and information sciences and such occupational fields as computer software engineering, computer systems analysts, computer information science, and network systems administrators. These skills are hard to train and can be hard to recruit and retain. They exist in larger numbers than the other two groups of skills, but industry demand for them can be "boom and bust," as the computer technology collapse of the last few years testifies. In 2001, the government projected that the demand for computer software engineers would grow by 100 percent over the period to 2010.[6] That projection now seems wildly optimistic. Yet, although IT specialists are now in more than ample supply, the boom phase of the cycle will return, so some planning for it is prudent.

In the near term beyond existing shortfalls, operations other than war and homeland security will drive additional personnel needs. After the end of the Cold War and Operation Desert Storm, the military was deployed from Somalia to Haiti and Bosnia in operations ranging from peacekeeping to disaster assistance to nation building. Not only will such operations continue, but their numbers will increase as so-called failed states risk humanitarian crises and may harbor terrorist threats. The skills required vary considerably, but it is likely that linguists and civil affairs and intelligence personnel will play a central role.

In the 1990s, the military recognized a need to begin addressing potential threats to the continental United States from chemical, biological, radiological, nuclear, and high-yield explosive attacks. That need was tragically underscored by the events of September 11, 2001. Consequently, homeland security activities are likely to require expertise that is not available in large numbers—for instance, explosives or chemical specialists and those with certain medical skills. Some of these skills, in medicine, for instance, do not easily become obsolete if not used, but others do. Although the precise skills and numbers will depend on the specifics of particular attacks, when they are needed, they will be needed quickly but episodically. Moreover, the crisis episodes during which they are most

---

[6]Daniel E. Hecker, "Occupational Employment Projections to 2010," *Monthly Labor Review*, November 2001, p. 62. Available at http://stats.bls.gov/opub/mlr/, last accessed June 9, 2003.

needed by the military will also be periods in which civilian society needs them most.

The future, including the personnel future, is very uncertain. Despite the predictability of some personnel needs, others will arise quickly from particular combinations of threats, emergencies, and technologies. In those circumstances, predicting personnel needs is like trying to bet on particular stock market outcomes. For investors in the stock market, the usual response is a diversified portfolio. For the RC, the ultimate challenge is to build enough flexibility to respond to needs that arise quickly with little warning.

Cutting-Edge Policy Initiatives

In thinking about how the military could best go about meeting this challenge, we examined a wide range of policy ideas. As enumerated above, we focused on five policy ideas that seem both worthwhile and feasible:

1.   Civilian Skills Database

2.   Expanded "Participating IRR"

3.   "Tailored" ESGR

4.   RC-Focused PaYS

5.   Critical University Talent Program.

We summarize these ideas in Table 1. We then discuss each in more detail, first giving a description of the idea and why it might have merit; then making preliminary judgments about what would have to change in law and practice to make it happen, who or what institution would have to make that change, how hard and expensive it would be, and how big a skill pool might be attracted. Because our judgments are preliminary, refining them with pilot projects or experiments would be the logical next step. At this stage, however, we excluded policy ideas if they seemed to require major changes in law (for instance, giving companies that cooperated with the RC an advantage in competitions for contacts) or dramatic changes in how the RC is managed (for instance, generalized provisions for lateral entry in mid-career), although many of those ideas merit consideration in the longer term.

1. Database of Skills Possessed by Existing RC Members, Especially Those in the IRR

What is it? The best place to start in harnessing skills in the RC is with the skills that are already present. But the databases used by RC managers generally

Table 1

Cutting-Edge Policy Ideas

	Program				
	Civilian Skills Database	Expanded Partici-pating IRR	"Tailored" ESGR	RC-Focused PaYS	Critical University Talent
Purpose	Identify existing RC members with cutting-edge skills	Encourage more IRR members to participate	Recruit critical skills through companies	Increase number of RC recruits by broker-ing connection to employers	Get critical university-based talent on retainer
Targets	All current RC members	IRR members, especially those with cutting-edge skills	Companies identified as cutting-edge	Non–prior service possible recruits	Federal-grantee university departments
Incentives	Pay for training period Retirement points "Yellow pages"	Pay Retirement points Other non-salary	? More-aggres-sive RC outreach to private sector	Only the chance to interview with companies	Stipends to graduate students and faculty
Yearly program costs	$20–30 million if training pay included	Very dependent on mix of incentives	$5–10 million	$2 million	$20 million for 100 retainers
Number of skill sets produced	4,000?	10,000?	?	? (15,000 might participate)	100?

NOTE: A question mark refers to uncertainties in this area.

contain, at most, the current civilian occupation of service members. They are lacking in three dimensions—timeliness (occupation information is rarely updated), history (only one occupation can be maintained in most databases), and skill-level depth (What kind of programs can this software engineer write? What kind of law does this lawyer practice?). So it is more than possible that a desired skill set might already be present, were that fact only known.

Why is it needed? Better databases could produce a relatively short-term "win-win" situation. Although the services are working on the problem, no comprehensive database currently exists. Each service has its own official database, often subdivided by component, and what data fields actually mean is often idiosyncratic, existing in the head of a long-time personnel manager. At the same time, most services are exploring databases to track civilian skills separately from the database of record. Rather than trying to create yet more databases, it probably makes more sense to make the databases as compatible with each other as possible.

What are the closest existing parallels? Joint Reserve Intelligence Planning Support System (JRIPSS); Army Reserve Civilian Acquired Skills Database (CASDB); Naval Reserve Skills Online (NRSO) Defense Integrated Military Human Resources System (DIMHRS).

What would have to change to make the program happen? The first change is technological: The system needs to be designed to allow tracking of a rich set of data on a service member's civilian skills within an official database. The JRIPSS/CASDB/NRSO software works well as a stand-alone system, so the major hurdle is designing the pipeline for the data to pass through to the official databases in a form that is useful for personnel management. The second change is behavioral: Service members need to be informed and persuaded about the system so that enough of them enter their personnel skills to make the system pay off. Part of the answer is to create a system of incentives for their immediate participation—registering themselves in the database and periodically refreshing their data. In addition, the reporting has to be done in a way that does not necessarily commit the member to using that skill. While some members might be eager to do so, others value their affiliation with the RC precisely because it is *not* what they do in civilian life, and would want to have a choice about how closely to link the two.

These two sets of changes are in fact linked. Service members will not contribute to a system that works poorly or is redundant with their official communication with personnel managers, and the services will not make the needed investment in the programs unless they are confident reservists will respond in sufficient numbers.

Who or what would have to make the change? Because the most effective and efficient way to implement both kinds of change is from the top down, the Office of the Secretary of Defense for Reserve Affairs (OSD [RA]) should take the lead in funding and directing the development of both the information system and the personnel incentives to make the proposals a reality. In the past, each component (as well as OSD) has voluntarily contributed money to the CASDB/NRSO/ JRIPSS program. Because the program will work best if the software is seamless across services, it seems to make sense for OSD to be the proponent and main sponsor of the work. (Each service may still want to contribute separately for work on the Internet interface or other unique aspects.)

Once OSD has provided the IT solution and the incentive options, the burden should shift to commanders at all levels to inform and motivate personnel to provide the needed data. This includes the reserve personnel center commanders who are responsible for each service's IRR, since the latter are in the category with the biggest "upside" to using civilian skills as the road to greater RC participation.

How hard (and expensive) is the change? Because the IT program is not a drastic innovation, it should be relatively affordable. The JRIPSS family of databases is already completed, and primarily needs to be maintained, at a cost of about $0.4 million per year. The DIMHRS project has anticipated this kind of capability from an early stage. The greatest challenge will be to develop the protocols and policies for data to flow to it from the legacy systems.

The net cost of incentives for service members would depend on the incentive and on the implication of locating an already-present skill set. Suppose there is a fairly generous incentive, one training period of pay, which is about $75 for an E-6 with 10 years of service. If 300,000 members of the Army Guard and Reserve provided input in a given year and received one training period of pay, the cost would be $22,500,000. At an estimated cost of $12,000 to bring one new recruit into the military from "off the street," that money could train 1,900 new personnel.[7]

So the program would pay for itself if 1,900 current personnel logging into the database were managed so as to put them on a new career path and replace the need to acquire and train an equal number of new personnel. Yet that could overstate savings in several ways. Personnel moving into positions requiring sought-after skills might still need some training for the military aspects of the new job. And the positions they vacated might still need to be filled, which would cost money even if those positions were not cutting-edge.

On the other hand, there would be hidden cost savings if the services or DoD effectively captured other information by means of on-line submissions from service members. Given the hundreds of thousands of dollars spent every year in mailing information to or calling personnel, any improvement in the existing databases' tracking of addresses, telephone numbers, and e-mail addresses could generate significant savings.

Perhaps less expensive, but presumably less attractive, would be for the services to offer a set number of retirement points to those who registered and updated

---

[7]Vince Crawley, "Pentagon Skeptical About 18-Month Enlistment Plan," *Army Times,* March 18, 2002, p. 10.

their data periodically. Although the costs of such a program are real, they would not come due until an RC member began collecting a reserve retirement payment. The relative cost and attractiveness of this incentive would have to be tested in a pilot project or experiment.

In the long run, however, the best incentive to ensure complete and accurate submission of skills information is the perception that doing so will lead to desirable opportunities for reservists, whether in uniform or through some link to civilian employers. Another incentive might be access to some portion of the entire database in return for updating their entries. For instance, if reservists were moving and wanted to locate a good dentist in a new location, they would have access to the database of civilian skills as a kind of "yellow pages." Giving cooperating employers access to the database could be another kind of incentive.

How large is the pool of talent that might be attracted by the change? Initial responses to the Internet-based stand-alone civilian skills databases have varied based on how strongly the leadership of each component pushed registration. The Navy Reserve officially commanded all members to enroll. The Army Reserve, which ran articles in its in-house magazine and mentioned registration in high-level briefings without requiring participation, had registered 32,000 of 340,000 members of the Ready Reserve by early 2003, with about another hundred signing up each day. In neither case was the service able to offer pay, retirement points, or other inducements to the service members. In the extreme, important milestones—like promotion or bonuses—could be made conditional on having updated one's entry.

2. Expanded "Participating IRR"[8]

What is it? This program, based on an existing Air Force program, would aim to identify, track, and reward a subset of IRR members who want to serve. They could be given particular incentives—perhaps pay, but also training opportunities or health, retirement, or other non-salary benefits, although some of these non-salary benefits, health care in particular, can be expensive. Particular cutting-edge skills, such as language or technology skills, might be

---

[8]In late 2002, two Pentagon offices, C4ISR and Personnel and Readiness, worked together to find ways to get access to one cutting-edge skill set, communications engineers. Three of the four ideas under consideration involved the RC, and, not surprisingly, all of those three were ones this project had considered. Two of them were nearly identical to two of the innovations considered in detail here. In the Pentagon's version of Participating IRR, called Controlled Specialty IRR, possessors of cutting-edge skills would not be required to train on weekends or perform the customary two-week annual reserve duty, but instead they would be asked to come on active duty for specific projects requiring their expertise.

special targets. Participating IRR members would not be counted against unit strengths or ceilings.

Why is it needed? At present, most IRR members are invisible and unaccounted for by RC management. Most of them want it that way because they are merely filling out the remainder of their eight-year service commitment after they have finished service with the AC or selected reserve. Yet a subset could be more active. Some members might, for particular reasons, not want to join the ranks of IMAs (Individual Mobilization Augmentees) but would welcome more active, albeit selective, participation in the RC.

What are the closest existing parallels? In all the services, there are IRR personnel who participate actively. In some cases, they are an amorphous group of "tour babies" on whom managers can count to volunteer for short assignments—and who draw pay for those assignments. Conversations with the various reserve personnel commands suggest that significant fractions of the IRR perform more than 15 days of active duty each year. Some of these volunteers are counted in a more clearly defined group, such as the Air Force Participating IRR (PIRR), which numbers some 2,700.

Even more structured is the IRR Activation Authority (IRRAA), enacted into law in 1998, under which IRR members agree to be subject to activation under Presidential Reserve Call-up. This authority has not lived up to the hoped-for levels of participation. For example, roughly 30,000 IRR members were expected to volunteer for the IRRAA. As of now, there are essentially no personnel in this program (a handful of names remain on the rolls but these personnel will soon complete their term of commitment to the IRR). One could characterize the IRRAA as a program with little appeal beyond patriotism. It offered the same risk of being called up under Presidential Selected Reserve Call-up (PSRC) authority as that experienced by members of the Selected Reserve, but with none of the benefits of Selected Reserve participation for the service members who volunteered for it.

What would have to change to make the program happen? Based on Air Force experience, the change could be fairly simple. It requires only creating the category, targeting it, and deciding on incentives. Expanding the Air Force Reserve PIRR programs and extending PIRR practices to the Army Reserve could minimize many of the complications associated with the IMA program.[9]

---

[9]*Air Force Instruction (AFI) 36-2633, The Air Force Reserve Individual Ready Reserve Program— Management and Mobilization,* outlines the procedures and standards required for managing the PIRR. The project's main point of contact has been Col. Erret ("Rett") Porter, HQ/ARPC/XPX. Joe Herbertson is the contact for IRR management and mobilization.

Who/what would have to make the change? Expanding the Air Force program would require a decision by the Chief of the Air Force Reserve to expand the scope of professional manning programs for the PIRR or to create new categories of professional manning programs that would target critical skills. Starting a PIRR in the Army would require a comparable decision by the Chief of the Army Reserve. Units would also have to accept the participants, but those participants would come nearly "free"—they would be only a very modest administrative burden (since they would continue to be managed by the relevant personnel center) and they would not count against strengths or ceilings.

How hard (and expensive) is the change? Expanding the program in the Air Force should take little if any increase in resources. The infrastructure and procedures appear to be in place to accommodate increased participation levels. Implementing a similar program in the Army will have start-up and maintenance costs associated with policy formulation, program awareness, and program management. To be sure, when members of a Participating IRR actually did duty, they would be paid for that time, so although organizing an expanded Participating IRR would be inexpensive, actual participation would carry costs.

The more significant cost to expanding IRR participation would be the implications for how the RC is currently managed. The participants might live far from the units that needed their skills; most units do not want to count on such people, and the military culture discourages it. More generally, while reservists are called up individually, the official practice is to call them as units, and expanding the participating IRR would require the RC to accept an individual form of participation on a much broader scale.

How big is the pool of those who might be interested? What would it take to interest them? The Air Reserve Personnel Center (ARPC) considers the approximately 2,700 IRR members—who participate as members of the Ready Reserve without pay but who receive points toward retirement—as the best source of personnel with critical skills to satisfy projected needs.[10] Currently, the IRR participation programs range from Military Personnel Appropriation tours for active-duty manning support, to the Ready Reinforcement Personnel Section program for transitory assignments, to specialized programs for recruiting chaplains and medical personnel and supporting the Civil Air Patrol program and Air Force

---

[10]"Special programs exist in the IRR that permit participation, under certain conditions, and on a voluntary basis. Generally, participation . . . is permitted for programs established by law, to satisfy professional manning and procurement programs, to permit continuation of training on a temporary basis while in assignment transition, and to fill validated but unfunded Selective Reserve positions." (*Air Force Instruction 36-2633, The Air Force Reserve Individual Ready Reserve Program—Management and Mobilization*, December 1, 1995, p. 3.)

Academy recruiting. Unit manpower or occupational specialty ceilings do not limit an IRR member's participation. Combined, these PIRR programs resulted in nearly 25,000 Military Personnel Appropriations (MPA) man-days in FY 2001. The structure and administration of the programs can accommodate the participation of a broader pool of non-IRR members with critical skills.

The ARPC reports that current PIRR programs are targeted to attract service from two types of IRR members: (1) those who either possess a specific professional occupational skill set (for instance, law, clergy, or health services); or (2) reservists who cannot find a Selected Reserve position and are willing to perform in units that require general or administrative skills (for instance, the Ready Reserve Personnel Section program). The level of interest of IRR personnel who possess critical skill sets is not yet known. Based on the experience of the Air Force, which, as mentioned, has 2,700 participating IRR members out of a total of about 60,000, the total pool for the Army, for instance, might be in the range of 7,000–8,000 (out of 150,000 IRR members).

The participating IRR might target and create special categories for people with specific cutting-edge skills. In that sense, it could be a low-cost way to build a pool of such talent. It could also be turned from a group of service members completing their obligations into a form of lateral entry. New entrants with targeted skills might find the participating IRR a congenial way to serve their country, and some might use it as a stepping stone to a still more active form of reserve service.

3. "Tailored" ESGR[11]

What is it? This program would build on the basic structure of the existing ESGR but would seek to foster more and better connections to employers, in an effort to draw cutting-edge skills into the military by means of employers. There is now a national mandate for greater action, as well as for better information.

Why is it needed? The Department of Defense needs to know where scarce occupational skills, critical to national security, exist in the general population and how to quickly integrate more people who possess those skills into the

---

[11]In 2002, the Pentagon's Corporate Partnerships idea combined features of our Critical University Talent Program and Targeted ESGR idea. Under the Corporate Partnerships program, the Pentagon would contract with companies, universities, or communities to provide people with cutting-edge skills. Companies, for instance, might be given outsourced contracts in return for committing to make a number of employees available for service in the Guard or Reserves. Those people might serve in or out of uniform, with the source of their compensation during their periods of military service to be worked out in individual agreements.

reserve components. A "tailored" ESGR built on ESGR's existing nationwide infrastructure could be a major contributor to fulfilling this need. The ESGR organization may provide the fastest and most effective means to access these critical, cutting-edge resources. It understands the constraints of both the employer's willingness and ability to contribute employees and the employee's willingness to participate.

Current ESGR programs and initiatives could be expanded to pursue the active commitment of targeted industry leaders and business executives to facilitate the RC participation of their employees who possess critical cutting-edge skills. In particular, ESGR could enhance the targeting of its message to specific geographical regions, industry sectors, and firms where critical skills reside. Its role would be to identify the location of specific critical skill talent pools that exist in industry sectors and specific firms within those sectors, and to develop comprehensive, targeted marketing strategies to industry leaders, business executives, and people possessing critical skills.

ESGR would work in concert with the recruiting commands to sign up people in the IRR through a variety of coordinated strategies. Critical-skill leads generated by local-level ESGR volunteers could be handed off to RC recruiters, and those recruiters would be integrated into ESGR programs such as "Bosslifts," "Briefings with the Boss," and "Employer Awards and Recognition Programs" to expand the program into a recruiting tool. The program might create a specialized recruiting cell staffed by service component recruiters to develop and execute strategic RC recruiting programs for acquiring critical skills. It would thus serve as the test bed for new civilian utilization programs that directly support gaining access to cutting-edge skills and initiate partnerships with firms that have employees who possess these skills.

What are the closest existing parallels? ESGR already exists.

What would have to change to make the program happen? The changes would be limited because the proposal is consistent with many of the changes already under way within ESGR. Such changes include its reconstitution of a national advisory body (Executive Committee) with sufficient stature to have credibility with business and agency leaders; its increased focus on marketing efforts targeted to employers; its effort to increase its ability to attract volunteers in the business sector to assist with business-to-business networking (which implies less dependence on recruiting military retirees as the primary volunteers and leaders); and its lessened focus on traditional activities and programs and increased emphasis on networking.

Who/what would have to make the change? In addition to the changes within ESGR, ESGR would need to form strategic partnerships with one or more organizations having complementary constituencies and missions—for instance, the Council for Excellence in Government (which promotes innovations in government and creative human capital initiatives) or Business Executives for National Security (BENS).[12] It would need to shape better ongoing communication with RC leaders at the national and state levels to determine needs and issues. It would also need more ability to gather and analyze data on employers of current National Guard and Reserve members and communicate electronically through Web-based channels. Finally, it would need to acquire the sophistication of its programs and events to be on par with the standards of corporate America.

How hard (and expensive) is the change? Based on ESGR estimates, the change at ESGR headquarters would be significant in reducing the "military" flavor of the organization and elevating sensitivity to business culture and issues. Six to 10 paid civilian staff from the corporate and/or private/nonprofit sectors, particularly with human resources, IT, or marketing backgrounds, would be needed. In addition, the program would need about 10 additional field staff (two per region) to handle referrals and screening of resumes, background checks, association presentations, and coordination with military reserve recruiters. All of these positions could be either contractors or "loaned executives" from industry.

For funding, a very rough estimate of costs would be in the range of $5–10 million per year. That might break down, again very roughly, into $0.6 million for improved promotional items, $1.2 million for better promotional events, $2 million for salaries, $0.5 million for IT enhancements such as email newsgroups and online "job boards," $1.6 million for more industry symposiums, $0.8 million for expanded travel to meet with both military and corporate stakeholders, and $0.5 million for expenses for ESGR corporate representatives.

How large is the pool of talent that might be attracted by the change? This is the key issue for consideration, and it is by nature difficult to estimate. The money involved is significant but not large, and in many senses this initiative would help ESGR move in the direction it should go in any case. That said, the opportunity cost in money and top-level attention is significant. The program might be started with particular industry sectors employing cutting-edge skills. As it grew, it would provide both experience and infrastructure for creating and testing new participation strategies that would facilitate participation by people

---

[12]We appreciate the assistance of Capt. Barton D. Buechner (USN) and Col. Alan R. Smith (USMC), and of their staffs, in this analysis.

who possess critical skills and facilitate support by their employers. For instance, employers might provide one person for 30 days, then another with similar skills for another 30 days. Or employees of different firms but with the same critical skills might participate in the IRR for consecutive short periods.

Next steps to refine the "tailored" ESGR idea could include

- establishing a "public/private partnership" task force to design workable program parameters
- creating a workable prototype organization with one to three existing ESGR committees to test some of these ideas
- forming a congressional panel with "emergency powers" to recommend legislative changes to remove barriers
- identifying several areas of "specialized expertise" where links to companies already exist, and experimenting with different forms of participation.

4. RC-Focused Program Modeled on PaYS

What is it? The Army PaYS program is a partnership between the Army and participating private-sector firms. It is designed to attract young people into the Army who are interested in obtaining high-quality civilian employment after serving their terms of enlistment. During their enlistment in the Army, soldiers learn technical skills required by industry along with work ethics, teamwork, communication, and leadership. After completing their active-duty tour, the soldiers transition to the company selected during the recruiting process. By analogy, a PaYS-like program would be created for the RC in which industry participants would agree to hire or give preference to members of the RC. In the program, the RC would maintain basic technical skills, discipline, and training.

For PaYS at present, a database that matches the job needs of a company with the 94 job skills offered by the Army enables the new recruit to choose a particular company and job skill. An agreement with a specific company that reflects the military skill, civilian job, and terms of service is prepared when the young person enlists. Individuals participating in the PaYS program are also eligible for other monetary and nonmonetary incentives to enlist in the Army. The PaYS program does not result in a guaranteed job for participants, but it does guarantee opportunities by giving participants the chance to interview with company human resources staff.

Why is it needed? Private-sector companies would benefit because PaYS would provide employers with a pool of talented and trained individuals with a variety of job skills that have direct application in the civilian sector. Reservists also bring discipline and professional accomplishments, and they have been screened and held to the highest standards of conduct. And employers save recruiting and training costs by participating.

The RC would benefit because enlisting in the RC would become more attractive given the PaYS corporate partners. The RC would then have access to a pool of talent without having to directly compete against employers for the same scarce resource. Additionally, the RC would gain valuable industry partners that acknowledge the RC as a quality producer of skilled employees.

What are the closest existing parallels? PaYS already exists for the AC.

What would have to change to make the program happen? Presumably, not much would have to change to create an RC-focused PaYS program. The Army is already developing a program for the RC. The main issue would be how to expand it to the other services.

PaYS for both the AC and the RC originated as a concept in 1999 in U.S. Army Recruiting Command (USAREC) because of projections that Army recruitment would fail to meet its requirement in the near future—by 25 percent in the case of the RC. The idea was that through partnerships with industry, the Army could work with industry, not compete against it—a natural idea for cutting-edge skills. The initiative was launched in June 2000, but the RC component was put on hold given the task of launching the AC component. The RC launch was October 2002.

Who/what would have to make the change? The main changes would come from an expansion of the idea to other services. USAREC is trying to make PaYS for the AC and RC seamless. Companies would sign one memorandum of agreement covering both the AC and RC, and they would then have the option of choosing whether they want ex-active-duty soldiers or reservists.

How hard (and expensive) is the change? USAREC anticipates that PaYS could be managed by four marketing analysts (two paid for by the RC and two by the AC). Together, the four would cost roughly $0.4 million per year. Of course, there would also be the opportunity cost of high-level attention, plus the organizational learning required to begin new programs in the other services.

How large is the pool of talent that might be attracted by the change? Although some companies—Dyncorp, for example—have indicated to the Army that they are interested only in people with a full active-duty tour because they want their hands-on experience, other companies are interested in reservists because of their training, discipline, work ethic, screening, and character. Five to six major companies are already looking into the reservist database. On the health care side, HCA and Johns Hopkins have expressed interest, particularly because of the training the military provides. For example, a licensed practical nurse in the RC would be sent to school by the Army for a year to become accredited. Employers are interested because they would not have to wait three to six years to hire these candidates as they do for those in the AC program.

The planned PaYS program for the RC is limited to non-prior-service reservists because USAREC believes that access to good jobs will help with recruitment. USAREC estimates that roughly 10,000–15,000 reservists would participate in a given year. Of course, this number refers to total participants; it leaves unclear (and a subject for surveying) how many actually joined the RC because of the PaYS incentive. On the AC side, the participant cap is 7,950, which is 10 percent of the accession goal. In 2002, there were 4,454 participating in the program. One limitation of PaYS is the need to find companies within 50 miles of service, and there are other requirements as well. But local knowledge can also be a help. For instance, Army reserve battalion commanders were asked to identify companies in their areas who would be good PaYS partners.

The AC-focused PaYS program has somewhat different incentives for companies from what an RC-focused PaYS program would have. In the AC-focused program, new service members become private-sector employees only after completing their terms of enlistment. So these hires bring a demonstrated history of training and accomplishment to their companies. This is not necessarily the case for new members of the RC, who may not have served previously in the AC. As a result, these members may not bring the same type of experience and training (at least immediately) to companies, and accordingly they may be less attractive candidates.

Another issue involves training and credentials in the RC. A participating company may require that an employee possess a credential issued by a nationally recognized organization or state licensing board. In many cases, the formal training that members in the RC receive for a Military Occupational Specialty translates directly to a civilian skill in the private sector. In other cases, however, the translation is indirect. It will be important for the RC to work with industry so that companies accept RC training certificates and equipment licenses to the greatest extent possible.

5. Critical University Talent Program

What is it? This new initiative would identify colleges and universities that employ faculty and produce graduates at the undergraduate and graduate levels who possess the cutting-edge skills that the military needs. It would identify a specific recruitment pool of faculty and students within these institutions who possess the state-of-the-art science and technical skills or the most current academic knowledge that is sought. It would then develop a retainer-based recruiting and retention program within the IRR to fulfill national security needs from this talent pool.

Why is it needed? Many of the nation's colleges and universities have a long history of producing cutting-edge technical innovations and comprehensive social and geopolitical insights for the federal agencies. These institutions are centers of highly skilled human capital for the nation. The DoD has also had a long history of finding ways to directly leverage the skills of university faculty, staff, and students to accomplish its missions through research grant and partnership programs.

Clearly, the nations' colleges and universities have the productive capacity to develop graduates with the critical skills that could successfully supplement DoD's projected needs. However, it will be a formidable challenge to find the people who possess those skills and attract them into some form of RC participation in spite of their preconceived notions about reserve duty or the market demands for the skills they possess. Increasing the RC's access to cutting-edge talent—and the nation's as well—will call for a more robust and highly targeted strategy for attracting people with these skill sets into service

Who/what would have to make the change? In 2001, the Congress earmarked an award of roughly $394 million to 126 public and private universities to perform DoD-supported basic and applied research in such areas as supercomputing, biotechnology, communications technology, disaster management, acoustics, and defenses against bioterrorism.[13] Some examples are shown in Table 2.

The DoD is not alone in funding university-based programs that employ and develop people who possess critical skills for national security. The Department of Education, for example, supports nationwide programs directed at foreign language study and foreign area study. The National Resource Center (NRC) and Foreign Language and Area Studies (FLAS) programs train specialists in modern

---

[13]The total amount that Congress earmarked as individual grants to support defense-related research at universities was $394,386,946, as reported by *The Chronicle for Higher Education:* http://chronicle.com/stats/pork/, last accessed June 9, 2003.

Table 2

Examples of Universities Receiving DoD Research Grants in 2001

Institution	Funding	Description
University of Alaska at Fairbanks	$30 million	For the university's Arctic Region Supercomputing Center to buy high-performance computer equipment
University of Alaska at Fairbanks	$4 million	For research related to predicting weather and the impact of the sun on electronic communications
University of South Florida	$3.5 million	For research to improve defenses against chemical and biological terrorism
University of Hawaii-Manoa	$5 million	To develop an imaging system for the detection and analysis of airborne particles that indicate the production, testing, or use of weapons of mass destruction
Drexel University	$1.2 million	For research to develop hybrid, fiber-optic-and-wireless communications systems
University of Texas at Austin	$2 million	For research to develop cannons that use electromagnets to fire projectiles

foreign language and area or international studies. NRC grants are awarded to institutions of higher education for the purpose of establishing, strengthening, and operating undergraduate or comprehensive (containing undergraduate, graduate, and professional components) centers focusing on language and area or international studies. Institutions receiving FLAS Fellowship allocations award fellowships to graduate students to support the acquisition of foreign language competence and area or international expertise.[14] A sampling of the 236 universities receiving NRC and FLAS grants to support existing programs in 2001 is shown in Table 3.

How hard (and expensive) is the change? The government-supported university programs described above have strategic value that extends beyond the direct purpose of performing basic research in science and technology. They also serve as a focal point for a specific network of faculty, students, and technicians who already possess the hard-to-train and hard-to-fill skill sets that will be of increasing importance to the military.

There are a variety of ways to recruit and retain talented individuals from these universities. One would be to conceive of those people as a pool of civilians who

---

[14]See http://www.ed.gov/offices/OPE/HEP/iegps/, last accessed June 9, 2003.

Table 3

Sample of Institutions Receiving Federal NRC and FLAS Grants

Institution	NRC Grant Recipient	FLAS Recipient	Amount
University of California, Los Angeles, James S. Coleman African Studies Center	√	√	$308,000
University of Florida, Center for African Studies	√	√	$314,000
Michigan State University, Asian Studies Center	√		$193,000
Stanford University, East Asia National Resource Center	√	√	$394,000
New York University, Center for Latin American and Caribbean Studies	√	√	$174,162
University of Texas, Institute of Latin American Studies	√	√	$327,271
Emory University, Middle Eastern Studies	√		$185,000
Georgetown University, National Resource Center for the Middle East	√	√	$233,000
University of Chicago, Center for Middle Eastern Studies	√	√	$361,000
University of Virginia, Center for South Asian Studies	√	√	$362,000
University of Hawaii, Center for Southeast Asian Studies	√	√	$352,246

could be quickly called on when needed, but only then. They would not enlist in the armed forces or be required to attend officer or enlisted basic training courses.

They would be volunteers with specific skills and paid a retainer fee over a three-year period of participation in a special (new) category of the IRR. Participants would sign a contract that would stipulate that they could be subject to being called on to work full-time for the federal government under PSRC authority for up to a one-year period.

If the majority of participants were graduate students at these universities, the retainer would need to be commensurate with other stipend alternatives available to them. Table 4 shows the range of some stipends for various disciplines at several schools.

These examples suggest a stipend range of $13,000–$20,000 annually, depending on the school and the specific discipline. The key uncertainty—again, a natural subject for a pilot project—is how much of a premium talented people in high-salary specialties might seek to offset the risk that they would be called to duty at pay beneath their expected civilian rate. Since the goal is to attract the best talent, not to meet per capita quotas, personnel managers should be allowed discretion in hiring and contracting just as most commercial firms do today—very different, certainly, from the government's structured and inflexible hiring rules.

How large is the pool of talent that might be attracted by the change? The staff, faculty, and students associated with the NRC and FLAS programs represent the potential pool. Their skill sets could be further segmented by proficiency level and identified by geographic location. We felt that it was premature to conduct interviews to sample interest among government-funded centers. However, the existing National Security Education Program (NSEP) is suggestive of the possible attractions. It was begun a decade ago, with support and funding through the intelligence committees of Congress, as a way to build U.S. capacity for dealing with unusual languages and distant, little-known cultures.[15] It subsidizes study in targeted subjects in exchange for commitments of subsequent government service. It currently funds 60–80 graduate students and 170–180 undergraduates, with stipends up to $10,000 per semester for overseas

Table 4

Stipends for Teaching and Research Assistants

School	Discipline	Teaching Assistant Stipend	Research Assistant Stipend
New York University	Economics	$18,000	
Princeton University	English	$17,500	
University of Virginia	Mechanical Engineering		$13,500
University of Maryland	Mechanical Engineering		$20,665
Texas A&M University	Biology		$15,300

SOURCE: "Stipends Are Key in Competition to Land Top Graduate Students," *The Chronicle of Higher Education,* September 28, 2001.

---

[15]See http://nsep.aed.org/facts.html, last accessed June 9, 2003.

study. This program is only suggestive, however, because the market for many, perhaps most, unusual languages has been thin and not well-paying.

Testing the Agenda

Table 1 on page 7 displays the differences among the five ideas and the uncertainties about their effects. The Critical University Talent Program, for instance, seems expensive for the talent it nets. But is it? It is impossible to know for sure without taking the logical next step: Conduct pilot tests of the policy ideas to gain a clearer sense of costs and benefits in terms of attracting desired skill sets. Ideally, these tests would be rigorous, with a control group or baseline to assess yield and cost with and without the new initiatives. Pilot-testing would be especially important for the newest ideas, such as the Critical University Talent Program. Otherwise, good ideas run the risk of being adopted or killed, willy-nilly, by temporary enthusiasms, political considerations, or constituencies that develop among particular universities or specialties.

The Army's 2+2+4 experiment suggests the shape of the testing.[16] In that experiment, the country was divided into three types of test cells based on geographic areas served by Army recruiting battalions. The three types were selected to resemble one another as much as possible: Each included areas in all parts of the country with similar ethnic and socioeconomic composition. One of the three sets of cells remained the baseline or control group. In our case, that would mean that no new policy idea would be implemented in one set.

The other two sets would then implement variants of the idea to test the key features. For the Expanded Participating IRR, the program might be implemented with pay in one area but only with non-salary benefits in the other. For the Critical Universities Talent Program, one set of cells might use a fixed stipend (or separate fixed stipends for graduate students and faculty) while the other set used a sliding scale based on some combination of the urgency of the military's need and the level of anticipated remuneration in the private sector. In both cases, the tests should indicate which variant of incentives seemed to perform better at attracting talent, especially the talent in greatest demand.

It is harder to construct a pilot project for Tailored ESGR because the program is less specific. In that case, perhaps prudence will confirm what cost might indicate: If Tailored ESGR were implemented in phases, those phases should be undertaken carefully and deliberately, with one set of test cells receiving the

---

[16]Richard Buddin and J. Michael Polich, *The 2+2+4 Recruiting Experiment: Design and Initial Results* (Santa Monica, CA: RAND, N-3187, 1990).

expanded program while the other(s) did not. The results would then provide some insight into whether the expanded version did better, and by how much.

Finally, testing should permit the ideas to be compared with each other, at least to some degree. Although the ideas have somewhat different targets, the process might begin by defining measures of merit common to all—some combination of person-days of service in cutting-edge skills jobs, new recruits attracted, skill sets available, and for how long—perhaps scored according to the urgency of the military's demand for them. The outcomes and costs of the various ideas could then be compared.

Along the way, other techniques could be used to shed light on remaining uncertainties. For instance, if the Army is right and at least 10,000 recruits take advantage of an RC PaYS program, was PaYS important in their decision to enlist or merely a nice opportunity once they were recruited? The Army may not yet know the answer. But it and the Pentagon should know before they expand the program or extend it to the other services.